Bush Theatre

WoLab

DREAMING AND DROWNING

by Kwame Owusu

Dreaming and Drowning premiered at the Bush Theatre, London,
in November 2023, produced by WoLab

DREAMING AND DROWNING

by Kwame Owusu

Cast

Malachi   Tienne Simon

Creative Team

Writer and Director   Kwame Owusu

Stage Manager   Aïsha Kent

Production Manager   Lisa Hood

Set and Costume Designer   Tomás Palmer

Sound Designer   Holly Khan

Lighting Designer   Joshua Gadsby

Movement Director   Ingrid Mackinnon

Dialect Coach   Mary Howland

For WoLab

Creative Director   Alistair Wilkinson

Producer   Sarah Allen

This production was funded by Arts Council England

Supported using public funding by
**ARTS COUNCIL
ENGLAND**

KWAME OWUSU

Kwame Owusu is a director and writer. He was the Resident Assistant Director at the Lyric Hammersmith, 2021/2022 and is a Young Associate at the Gate Theatre.

His work in theatre as a director includes: *The Bacchae* (Lyric Hammersmith); *Othello* (ArtsEd); *stoning mary* (Arts University Bournemouth); *The Wolf from the Door* (John Thaw Studio); *Rota* (Antwerp Mansion); *Pomona* (Edinburgh Festival Fringe/King's Arms, Manchester).

Work as a Staff Director includes: *Romeo and Julie* (National Theatre/ Sherman Theatre).

Work as an assistant director includes: *Closer*, *Britannicus*, *Scandaltown*, and *Running With Lions* (Lyric Hammersmith); *Bee* (Old Vic); *Utopolis* (Manchester International Festival).

Writing for audio includes *The Factory* for English Touring Theatre. Writing for theatre includes *HORIZON* for the Bush Theatre. He trained at the University of Manchester and Birkbeck, University of London.

TIENNE SIMON

Tienne Simon recently finished shooting one of the lead roles (Royce) in the Barnaby Roper feature film *Animal* opposite Eddie Marsan, Sam Claflin and Burn Gorman. Last year he shot one of the lead roles (Bishop) in Theresa Ikoko's BBC series *Grime Kids* which will come out towards the end of 2023. Tienne graduated from LAMDA in 2022.

AÏSHA KENT

Aïsha Kent is a stage manager and theatremaker. Recent SM credits include: *#Black Is* (Company 3); *Queer Folio* (1623 Theatre Company); Talawa Firsts, 2023. Producer and performer for Poetry Brothel London, a current, immersive performance art night.

Aïsha is passionate about creating work championing underrepresented people and communities. She does creative access work with disabled artists, theatre companies and makers, including Access All Areas and Graeae. She trained at Kent Uni and more recently completed an MA in Collaborative Theatre Making at Rose Bruford, winning the Change Maker Award from Bernardine Evaristo for being an exemplar in inclusion and diversity.

LISA HOOD

Lisa Hood trained in Theatre Arts at Middlesex University. After beginning her career working in various technical departments in theatres across London she worked as a freelance stage manager where notable credits include *An Octoroon* (Orange Tree) and *Jess and Joe Forever* (UK Tour).

Lisa further developed her technical skills at the Orange Tree Theatre where she joined in 2017 as Production Technician and from 2019 became Technical and Production Manger.

Production Manager credits for the Orange Tree include: *The Double Dealer*, *Little Baby Jesus*, *Amsterdam*, *Can't Wait for Christmas!*, *Out of Water*, *The Mikvah Project*, *Inside/Outside Festival*, *Shaw Shorts*, *Rice*, *Tom Fool*, *The False Servant*, *The Solid Life of Sugar Water* and *Duet For One*.

As a freelance Production Manager, selected credits include: *The Flying Dutchman* (Opera Up Close, UK tour); *My Uncle is Not Pablo Escobar* (Brixton House); *Woodhill* (LUNG Theatre); *Macbeth* (ETT Tour); *Northanger Abbey* (Orange Tree).

TOMÁS PALMER

Tomás Palmer is a Scottish/Brazilian designer who creates work for theatre, new writing, dance, opera, musicals and film. Tomás trained at the Glasgow School of Art and the Royal Welsh College of Music and Drama. He is one of the 2021 winners of The Linbury Prize for Stage Design and was the production designer on the BAFTA and BIFA Award winning short film *Too Rough* in 2022.

Theatre design credits include: *Blue Mist* (Royal Court); *The Bacchae* (Lyric Hammersmith); *Julius Caesar* (co-costume design with Rosanna Vize, RSC); *My Uncle is Not Pablo Escobar* (Brixton House); *Sanctuary* (Access All Areas); *Sophocles' Oedipus/silent practice* (LAMDA); *The Wellspring* (co-design with Rosie Elnile, Royal and Derngate); *Time is Running Out* (Gate Theatre, Cardiff); *Winning* (Glasgow School of Art); *Autocue* (Centre for Contemporary Art Glasgow).

Associate design credits include: *The Cherry Orchard* (Yard, ETT, HOME Manchester); *Sound of the Underground* (Royal Court).

HOLLY KHAN

Holly Khan is a British/Guyanese composer, sound designer and multi-instrumentalist, creating scores for theatre, film and installation.

Most recent theatre work includes: the Olivier-nominated *Blackout Songs*, *Biscuits for Breakfast* (Hampstead); *Duck* (Arcola); *The Invincibles* (Queen's Theatre Hornchurch); *Unseen Unheard* (Theatre Peckham); *Jules and Jim* (Jermyn Street); *Mansfield Park* (The Watermill); *The Beach House* (Park); *For A Palestinian* (Bristol Old Vic/Camden People's Theatre – OFFIE nominated for Best Sound Design); *Amal Meets Alice* (Good Chance Theatre Company, The Story Museum); *Kaleidoscope* (Filskit Theatre Company, Southbank Centre/Oxford Playhouse); *Ticker* (Alphabetti Theatre, Newcastle/Underbelly, Edinburgh/Theatre503).

Film and installation work includes: *Becoming An Artist: Bhajan Hunjan* (Tate Kids); *One Day* (Blind Summit Theatre, Anne Frank Trust); *Sanctuary* (Limbic Cinema, Stockton Arts Festival); *Song for the Metro* (The Sage Music Centre, Newcastle); *It's About Time* (UN Women/Battersea Arts Centre/Mayor of London); *Their Voices* (RAA/Global Health Film Festival, Barbican).

JOSHUA GADSBY   LIGHTING DESIGNER

Joshua Gadsby is a Lighting Designer and creative collaborator working across theatre, dance and live art. He regularly co-designs set, costume, and lighting with designer Naomi Kuyck-Cohen.

Lighting designs include: *New Beginning* (Queen's Theatre Hornchurch); *Mom, How Did You Meet The Beatles* (CFT); *Who Killed My Father* (Tron & UK Tour); *The Beauty Queen of Leenane* (Theatre by the Lake); *Alice in Wonderland* (Mercury, Colchester); *Gulliver's Travels* (lighting co-design, Unicorn); *Robin Hood: Legend Of The Forgotten Forest* (Bristol Old Vic); *Cat On A Hot Tin Roof* (Leicester Curve and ETT Tour); *in a word* (Young Vic); *A Kettle of Fish* (Yard); *The Tyler Sisters*, *Alligators* (Hampstead); *Still Ill* (New Diorama/Kandinksy); *As We Like It*, *Dragging Words*, *In Good Company* (The Place); *RISE: Macro vs. Micro* (Old Vic New Voices).

Co-designs include: *The Winston Machine* (New Diorama); *There Is A Light That Never Goes Out: Scenes From The Luddite Rebellion* (Royal Exchange); *Trainers* (Gate); *Dinomania* and *Trap Street* (also Schaubühne, Berlin) both for Kandinsky theatre at the New Diorama.

INGRID MACKINNON   MOVEMENT DIRECTOR

Theatre credits include: *The Choir Boy* (Bristol Old Vic); *Shooting Hedda Gabler* (Rose); *The Effect* (National) *Tina: The Tina Turner Musical* (Aldwych); Regents Park Season Associate: Intimacy Support 2023/2022: *La Cage Aux Folles*, *Robin Hood*, *The Tempest*, *Every Leaf a Hallelujah, Once on This Island, Antigone, 101 Dalmatians, Legally Blonde, Carousel, Romeo and Juliet; The Meaning of Zong* (Barbican/ Bristol Old Vic/UK Tour); *Blue* (ENO); *Further than the Furthest Thing* (Young Vic); *Trouble in Butetown* (Donmar); *Es & Flo* (Wales Millennium Centre/Kiln); *Phaedra* (National); *Super High Resolution* (Soho); *Enough of Him* (National Theatre of Scotland); *A Dead Body in Taos* (Fuel Theatre); *The Darkest Part of the Night, Girl on an Altar* (Kiln); *Playboy of the West Indies* (Birmingham Rep); *Moreno* (Theatre503); *Red Riding Hood* (Stratford East); *Antigone* (Mercury, Colchester); *Liminal – Le Gateau Chocolat* (King's Head); *Liar Heretic Thief* (Lyric Hammersmith); *Reimagining Cacophony* (Almeida); *First Encounters: The Merchant Of Venice, Kingdom Come* (RSC); *Josephine* (Theatre Royal Bath); *Typical* (Soho); *#WeAreArrested* (Arcola/RSC); *The Border* (Theatre Centre).

MARY HOWLAND   DIALECT COACH

Mary Howland started working as a dialect teacher and coach twenty years ago. Until a couple of years ago, she was combining production coaching with drama school teaching, at schools including the Birmingham School of Acting, the Royal Central School, RADA, and twelve years at LAMDA.

This has given her experience of working with a lot of actors, with a range of learning styles, on different styles of production, from Shakespeare to musicals.

Her theatre coaching work has included: *Much Ado about Nothing, The Mysteries* (Shakespeare's Globe); *An Octoroon* (National), and *Rutherford and Son, Standing at the Sky's Edge* (Sheffield Crucible).

A speciality of Mary's work for the last ten years has been with non-native English speakers, most notably Raphael Acloque (*The Great, Catherine the Great, Little Birds*), and with the non-English speaking actors in *The Spanish Princess,* working quickly on making their delivery of English lines clear and expressive.

ALISTAIR WILKINSON   CREATIVE DIRECTOR, WOLAB

Alistair Wilkinson is a highly-experienced, multiple award-winning, published, trans non-binary, queer, working class and disabled artist. They trained at Royal Central School of Speech and Drama, as well as on the Royal Court's Invitation Writers Group, and also completed an MA at RADA/Birkbeck. In the past they have made work for organisations such as the BBC, Punchdrunk, Sky TV, the National Theatre, the Old Vic, Barbican Centre, Shoreditch Town Hall, Arcola Theatre, and Curious Monkey. They have just been appointed as the first ever Creative Lead at the National Football Museum in Manchester; and are the former Head of Artist Development at the Old Vic; and recently finished leading on talent development at Punchdrunk. Their work at Punchdrunk won the company the Business of the Year from the Royal Borough of Greenwich, and also Partner of the Year from Greenwich University. Alistair is an Associate Artist at the National Youth Theatre, a Connect Artist for RTYDS, a trustee for Boundless, and a script reader for the Bush Theatre, Theatre503, Theatre Uncut, and the Papatango Prize.

SARAH ALLEN   PRODUCER, WOLAB

Sarah Allen is a producer from Somerset currently based in London. Her work frequently focuses on expanding the practice of producing with an emphasis on wellbeing, collaboration, community-building, and access. She also regularly works as an access support worker for artists working in theatre. In 2020 she graduated from The Royal Central School of Speech and Drama with an MA Distinction in Creative Producing, and has gone on to specialise in producing and fundraising for first time writers, directors, and performers.

Recent theatre work includes: *Vitamin D* (national tour); *Ladyfriends* (Hope Mill, Shakespeare North Playhouse); *Fame Whore* (King's Head Theatre); *All The Happy Things* (Theatre503); *Drop It* R&D (Lighthouse Poole); *Acid's Reign* (VAULT Festival 2023); *Juniper and Jules* (Soho Theatre).

WoLab

WoLab is a working laboratory for artists to create. WoLab trains, mentors, nurtures, and creatively entitles artists, helping them discover and refine their talents, and then showcases those talents to the industry. Recent work includes *ENG-ER-LAND* by Hannah Kumari; *For A Palestinian* by Bilal Hasna and Aaron Kilercioglu; and *RAINER* by Max Wilkinson. In Spring 2023, WoLab previewed Naomi Obeng's thrilling London debut, *We'll Be Who We Are* at VAULT Festival.

Other work in development includes: *Screwdriver* by Eve Cowley and Elin Schofield; *A Romantic Comedy* by Tiwa Lade; *TIGER* by Tom Kelsey; *Hot Rain in Hackney* by Alistair Wilkinson. Past work includes: *First Commissions* (Paines Plough); *The Actor-Writer Programme* (Theatre N16/Bunker Theatre); *Man-Cub* (RADA/King's Head); *PlayList* (King's Head); *happy ever after?* (Bunker Theatre); *In the Net* (Jermyn Street); and R&D's of *heavymetalsexyanimal* by Sam Rees (Theatre Deli); *a nightmare is witchwork* by Billie Collins (City of London School for Girls/ Pendleton College) and *Asperger's Children* by Peter Machen (Trinity Laban).

Bush Theatre

We make theatre for London. Now.

Opened in 1972, the Bush is a world-famous home for new plays and an internationally renowned champion of playwrights. We discover, nurture and produce the best new writers from the widest range of backgrounds from our home in a distinctive corner of west London.

The Bush has won over 100 awards and developed an enviable reputation for its acclaimed productions nationally and internationally. We are excited by exceptional new voices, stories and perspectives – particularly those with contemporary bite which reflect the vibrancy of British culture now.

Located in the renovated old library on Uxbridge Road in the heart of Shepherd's Bush, the Bush continues to create a space where all communities can be part of its future and call the theatre home.

bushtheatre.co.uk

Bush Theatre

Bush Theatre, 7 Uxbridge Road, London W12 8LJ
Box Office: 020 8743 5050 | Administration: 020 8743 3584
Email: info@bushtheatre.co.uk | bushtheatre.co.uk

Alternative Theatre Company Ltd
The Bush Theatre is a Registered Charity
and a company limited by guarantee.
Registered in England no. 1221968 Charity no. 270080

THANK YOU

The Bush Theatre would like to thank all its supporters whose valuable contributions have helped us to create a platform for our future and to promote the highest quality new writing, develop the next generation of creative talent, lead innovative community engagement work and champion diversity.

MAJOR DONORS

Charles Holloway
Jim & Michelle Gibson
Georgia Oetker
Tim & Cathy Score
Susie Simkins
Jack Thorne

SHOOTING STARS

Jim & Michelle Gibson

LONE STARS

Jax & Julian Bull
Clyde Cooper
Charles Holloway
Anthony Marraccino & Mariela Manso
Jim Marshall
Georgia Oetker
Susie Simkins

HANDFUL OF STARS

Charlie Bigham
Judy Bollinger
Sue Fletcher
Simon & Katherine Johnson
Joanna Kennedy
Garry Lawrence
Vivienne Lukey
Aditya Mittal
Sam & Jim Murgatroyd
Martha Plimpton
Bhagat Sharma
Dame Emma Thompson

RISING STARS

Martin Blackburn
David Brooks
Catharine Browne
Lauren Clancy
Tim Clark
Richard & Sarah Clarke
Susan Cuff
Matthew Cushen
Kim Evans
Mimi Findlay
Jack Gordon
Hugh & Sarah Grootenhuis
Thea Guest
Sarah Harrison
Uzma Hasan
Lesley Hill & Russ Shaw
Ann Joseph
Davina & Malcolm Judelson
Mike Lewis
Lynette Linton
Michael McCoy
Judy Mellor
Caro Millington
Kate Pakenham
Mark & Anne Paterson
Stephen Pidcock
Miguel & Valeri Ramos Handal
Karen & John Seal
James St. Ville KC
Peter Tausig
Joe Tinston & Amelia Knott
Jan Topham

CORPORATE SPONSORS

Biznography
Casting Pictures Ltd.
Nick Hern Books
S&P Global
The Agency
Wychwood Media

TRUSTS & FOUNDATIONS

Backstage Trust
Buffini Chao Foundation
Christina Smith Foundation
Daisy Trust
Esmée Fairbairn Foundation
The Foyle Foundation
Garfield Weston Foundation
Garrick Charitable Trust
Hammersmith United Charities
The Harold Hyam Wingate Foundation
Jerwood Arts
John Lyon's Charity
Martin Bowley Charitable Trust
The Thistle Trust
The Weinstock Fund

And all the donors who wish to remain anonymous.

Supported by
ARTS COUNCIL ENGLAND

If you are interested in finding out how to be involved, please visit **bushtheatre.co.uk/support-us** email **development@bushtheatre.co.uk** or call **020 8743 3584**.

Special thanks to:

Tienne Simon
Alistair Wilkinson
Sarah Allen
Tomás Palmer
Holly Khan
Aïsha Kent
Ingrid Mackinnon
Joshua Gadsby
Lisa Hood
Gabriel Clark
Imogen Sarre
Ingrid Selburg
Deirdre O'Halloran
Lynette Linton
Daniel Bailey
Mojisola Adebayo
Aaron Kilercioglu
Elander Moore
Ashley Byam
Emanuel Vuso
Tristan Fynn-Aiduenu
Anthony Simpson-Pike
Evangeline Cullingworth
Sarah Jane Schostack
Nikhil Parmar
Holly Rose Hawgood
Kit Withington
Sophia Griffin
Beru Tessema

DREAMING AND DROWNING

Kwame Owusu

To my mother, Naluwembe Binaisa.

Thank you for your infinite inspiration, courage, imagination, and love.

'The sea had jeeringly kept his finite body up, but drowned the infinite of his soul.'

Herman Melville, Moby-Dick *or* The Whale

'Who's there?'

William Shakespeare, Hamlet

'Something's in the water. I think there's something in the water.'

Kojey Radical & Mahalia, 'Water'

'I'll tell you what freedom is to me. No fear.'

Nina Simone

Character

MALACHI, *nineteen. Black. MLE accent.*

Note to Creatives and Actors

There are two worlds in this play: 'Nightmare' and 'Reality'. 'Nightmare' takes the form of Malachi's bedroom stranded at the bottom of the ocean. 'Reality' takes the form of Malachi's day-to-day existence. During the play, his anxiety worsens and a beast grows in the ocean – trying to break down the walls between 'Nightmare' and 'Reality', and consume Malachi. Over the course of the play, the water begins to bleed through these beast-induced cracks in the walls. Threatening to drown Malachi permanently, and make him prey for the beast.

This play is written for one actor. All additional characters should be fully and vividly embodied. Use everything at your disposal – different accents, voices, physicality – to make the characters as distinct as possible.

Embrace the strangeness of this world. Embrace the surreal, the joy, and the anxiety.

Be sonically and visually bold.

A dash (–) is used to mark an interruption – either by another character or Malachi interrupting himself.

Three asterisks (***) are used to make a scene transition (i.e. a change of time and/or location).

This text went to press before the end of rehearsals and so may differ slightly from the play as performed.

MALACHI *is trapped in his bedroom at the bottom of the ocean.*

He is underscored by a soundscape deep from the ocean.

He begins, urgent and anxious.

I'm drownin.

Drownin under seas like heavy lava on my skin

Meltin my insides inside out *inside*

I'm fallin fadin down into the damp

From open air to liquid blue, cold hue, where my lungs are heavy, thick, I'm drownin

Drownin, sinkin, four walls surroundin

Under under, I'm drownin

Drownin under blue and clutchin my throat fillin up upside *down*

I'm turnin, blood rushin to my head

Legs like lead sinkin, thrashin gaspin

Lungs contractin, cracked

I'm drownin

Drownin under waves crashin miles above eyes

I see nothin but murky grey shiftin fadin fallin out of sight with my mind losin light

I'm tryna kick up, push down, get up, breathe

Ocean ocean pushin down on me

I'm sinking

I'm falling

I'm drownin under blue my body's thrashin, kickin, gaspin,
    gaspin

He gasps for air.

***

I wake up gasping for air from a mad terrifying dream

A nightmare

A nightmare I've had every single night for the last four weeks.

And it's like –

First bad dream you're like alright cool

Get up, glass of water, go sleep –

Easy.

But then it comes *back*.

One night, two nights, three nights –

I start countin

Five nights, six nights

I keep countin

Eight nights, nine nights

Try ignore it

Ten nights, twelve nights

Keep tryna ignore it

Twenty nights, thirty nights later

Get here, go sleep, and have the same nightmare *again*.

Dreamin I'm drownin in my bedroom at the bottom of the ocean

Then I wake up –

Thick water slippin through my mind's eye

Tryna shake it off

Tryna shake off a dream

Tryna shake off a dream I was so sure would stop when I got
   to uni.

I'm in this greyed-out-flat-pack-too-tight room

Which is nothin like it looked like on the website

And I didn't realise but official arrival day's tomorrow, not
   today

So I'm on my ones

Waitin

Waitin for a hundred strangers and not gonna lie –

I'm nervous.

Like I'm excited and whatever but really and truly

I haven't had to make new friends since Year 7

I haven't had to make new friends since man were pourin ice
   over their heads

And puttin it on *Facebook*.

Like – it's been a long time.

And it was so much easier when I was eleven

I swear everything's easier when you're eleven

Sat next to this guy –

Femi

In Maths and English and French cos our surnames began with
the same letter

And we clicked like *that*.

And it was ideal cos I couldn't do algebra for shit

So he'd let me copy his answers before class

I was sick at English

I helped him back

And yeah... not gonna lie we were both shit at French

But we were a team, man.

Like me and him against the world type shit!

Like –

Couple months in we're playing ball

And we played football every single break

Him on the wing

Me up top

He'd deliver, I'd score

Like clockwork.

But this one time

He passes me the ball

And

I dunno

I dunno!

I was down *bad* that day!

I take a touch

Shoot

And I was so sure I was bout to be carried round the pitch in triumph

Like –

I had it!

Except…

I didn't have it.

It went wide right of the post and straight through the wing mirror of the head of form's car

Mr Wilson

And everyone's like –

'OHHHHHH MYYYYYY' –

Cos you know when somethin breaks at school?

When *anythin* breaks at school –

Pandemonium.

Drop a plate in the canteen whole room goes *mad*

For no reason.

Like why are you being so loud for??

So a ball hittin a teacher's car…?

My ear drums are *still* recoverin.

So I'm lookin left and right for Mr Wilson

Mr Wilson

Six-foot-five-ex-marines-clean-shaven-never-happy

So rule one of school –

Don't fuck with Mr Wilson

Just don't do it

And it must've been like what

Three seconds?

Wilson comes *chargin* out of school –

Must've had some sixth sense for anyone touchin his car

And he's like

(*Glasgow accent*.) 'WHO HAS DONE THAT TO MY CAR?
    WHO?!'

Shit.

But obviously I'm an honest guy

So I'm about to put my hand up

But then Femi pipes up tryna say it's on him

But I'm like no no sir it was me

So the whole thing turnin into some proper fuckin I am
    Spartacus shit, yeah

But Wilson's not liking this

Eyes expandin

Fist contractin

He's like –

'Both of youse! In. My. Office. Now'

We both follow.

Femi gives me a little nod as we walk inside

And yeah… we got detention for the rest of the week

But it didn't matter

At all

Cos he has my back

Had my back

And that's all I want here.

I'm on a fuckin mission, man.

Find my people

Find my lifelong people

Maybe even fall in love you know

I just wanna start again.

New chapter, new people, fresh start, like –

That's it

That's all I want

And you know, yeah

It's probably gonna be a *lot* –

But I'm excited.

Nervous

Yes

Shitting it

Also yes

But –

Excited.

And... so fuckin tired.

So lemme try sleep.

He breathes in.

He breathes out.

The sun rises.

***

Whole morning of a silence

And I'm thinking imma die here alone

Probably suffocatin in grey

Until *finally* I hear suitcase wheels

Footsteps on the corridor floor

I think about pokin my head round –

Say hi

But I'm not tryna be awkward

Locked in convo about fuckin trains and traffic cos I got no clue
what else to say

So I wait

I wait

Dig through boxes strainin under books and books I love

Octavia Butler, N.K. Jemisin, Tomi Adeyemi

Endless Black sci-fi and fantasy bound in spines

Kingdoms collapsing under distant skies

Crystallised in ink.

I dig through books for uni –

I open *Their Eyes Were Watching God* by Zora Neale Hurston

I read and read

Go on a walk

I read

Take a look at the SU guide

Circlin societies

And finally –

The evening comes.

***

I step inside this low-light-low-ceiling-high-stakes first attempt
at formin lifelong connections

Edge past a group of people already chattin

Feelin like I'm failin

Take a sip of fluorescent orange which I guess like is Fanta and
somethin

I don't even know

But it's really fuckin strong

Too strong –

I back it

Take another drink

Look around the room already formin introducin laughin chattin
addin socials

Take another sip

Sweat starts poolin

(*Laura, Derry accent.*) 'Hey, you okay?'

I look up and there's this girl

Shoulder-length blonde hair, green eyes, and bare freckles,
smilin right at me

'What? Yeah, yeah I'm good,' I say.

'I'm Laura!'

She says pointing at herself, bringin me into the group's orbit.

'Malachi.'

'This is Richard'

She says pointin towards –

A Fred Perry polo with grease layered thick across his hair

He flattens his mouth and does a kinda wave thing

'And this is Emily'

She says lookin to her left at –

A massive grin balancing on top of bright-green dungarees

(*Emily, Geordie accent.*) 'You alright!'

That's Emily

(*Laura*) 'What course are you on?'

That's Laura

'I –'

(*Laura*) 'Wait no let me guess! Uh… Mechanical Engineeering? No! Uh Sports Science?'

'English Lit'

(*Emily*) 'No way, me too!'

(*Richard, Essex accent.*) 'I think you're the only guy in here who's not an engineer'

That's Richard – kinda smilin not smilin.

(*Awkwardly laughs.*) 'Yeah, I'm not a numbers guy'

(*Emily*) 'Me neither! Why bother? Don't need Pythagoras to write a fuckin email do I?'

(*Genuinely laughs.*) 'Literally! Can't long-divide your way through life'

'And what, you can get through life with a book?'

'Yeah man, novels, poems –'

(*Laura*) 'Or history!'

'Yeah yeah or history. Is that what you do, Laura?'

(*Laura*) 'Yeah. Medieval though, so it's not that cool. But I love it.'

'Nah that's cool. And Richard you're…'

(*Richard*) 'An engineer… yeah. Mechanical.'

At this point Richard's not even smilin not smilin, he's just kinda grimacin

Grippin his beer so tight it's gonna pop –

(*Emily*) 'You comin out?'

'Of course! I can't wait!'

I say, tryna seem as excited and friendly as humanly possible.

(*Emily*) 'You're gonna love it, the music is literally *champion*!'

An hour passes. I take one too many shots, knowin I'm forcin it,
    but hopin I'm making a good impression.

***

*Sound plays. Somewhere in the mix is the unmistakeable sound
of 'Mr Brightside'.*

I step in

Kinda waved

Through a haze of Lynx Africa and sweat.

The light keeps shiftin

Turnin

The music despite Emily's promises is not 'champion'

It's actually very, very terrible.

We take a shot

Then another

And another

Laura and Emily charge forwards cuttin tracks through the
    crowd

Richard goes off to try chat up some girl

I'm frozen for a sec then try follow

But their path's sealed up shut behind them

I turn

The light turns

Twists round sweaty bodies

Blood vessels strainin in the heat

Everyone's kinda jumpin on the spot with no rhythm
  whatsoever.

But I look to my left and there's this guy

He's kinda cute

He's kinda blurry

I walk up towards him and before I know it my lips are on his
  lips his hands around my waist

I'm thinkin this is actually a pretty good kiss

He holds me tight, puts his tongue into my mouth, and it tastes
  like sick and feels like fur

Ohmygod

Like there's some kinda bacterial-next-pandemic-type-virus
  cookin up under his tongue.

Ohmygod!

I squeeze outta his dead man's grip

Carve a path towards white neon

Move straight for the toilet

Bend my head down and wait.

Nothing comes.

I leave the cubicle, open the door, tryna find the way out.

I turn, the light turns

I turn, the room turns –

Sweat

Wet

White

Washed

Sticky jumpin lights flashin gurnin lights flashin white washed
sticky heads thrashin 'Mr Brightside' comes on for the
fourteenth time

I need to cut.

I move towards the exit

But I bump into Emily by the bar and she's flickin through her
camera roll

Waiting to order

I say hey even though I just wanna go

And she shows me her phone, grinnin – tryna share the joke

I take a look and in amongst the videos of her and Laura dancin
and screamin at the camera –

There's me.

Me and that guy from before.

And I'm like what where's that from?

And she's gigglin and swayin

'I took it, obviously'

'Yeah okay why, I don't –'

'It's like a video diary! I do this like one-second-a-day thing
where –'

'Alright cool, but I don't wanna be in it like that'

She tries sayin it's funny.

'It's what uni's all about man –'

'Can you delete it', I say.

She says no.

'Delete it', I say

She says *why*

'It's not funny, it's just weird, I'm askin you to delete it, just –'.

'Alright don't shout'

'I'm not shoutin'

'It's literally just a joke, I wasn't gonna put it anywhere'

'I wasn't sayin you were gonna put it anywhere –'

'Good, cos I wasn't'

She keeps cuttin me off.

'It doesn't matter anyway, it's not deep', she says, lookin so
  confused and fed up

Like properly pissed off

And she sighs and rolls her eyes and deletes it and I leave

Chest tight, trust vanishin

Heart movin like a hummingbird

I race through the heavy dark –

Homeward.

***

I don't wanna be here.

I wanna be sixteen in the park gettin drunk and chattin shit

I wanna be at carni in the summer sun

I wanna be in my kitchen eatin ebinyebwa, luwombo, chapati,
  and mandazi

I wanna be thirteen in Westfield stockin up on free pretzel

I wanna be in my room hearin my mum blast Prince through the
    walls

But I'm not, I'm here, I'm here and –

MALACHI *is interrupted by a loud thud through the ceiling
above him.*

MALACHI *looks up and walks around the perimeter of the
room, listening intently.*

He hears nothing.

I try shake off what I'm feeling –

Close my eyes and brace

Gettin ready to duck –

Dive underneath the choppy surface and into deeper blue

Into the depths of a dream

I take a deep breath and another breath and I fall asleep and –

MALACHI *takes a deep breath.*

Darkness and the rush of the ocean fill the room.

***

MALACHI *is trapped in his bedroom at the bottom of the
ocean.*

I'm drownin

Drownin under seas like heavy lava on my skin

Meltin my insides inside out *inside* I feel like something's
    getting closer

Something's getting closer in the water

Shiftin divin duckin out of sight –

Claws wrappin reachin through the night –

Moves like light shiftin –

Closer

Like fiction no friction –

Closer

Divin through the blue

Divin through the dark

Divin through the deep dark, down

A salivating gullet and a wide open mouth

I'm thrashin kickin gaspin gaspin

MALACHI *gasps for air.*

***

I wake up and I'm rattled

Squeezin my eyes shut tryna remember every bit of my dream

Cos for the first night, in thirty-one nights there was something
different.

Something there.

Something in the water, something alive in the water.

I jump in the shower, full blast – tryna wash it off –

I get dressed and I head out.

***

I'm queuin outside the seminar room

Waitin

Waitin to be let in

Grippin my copy of *Their Eyes Were Watching God* by Zora Neale Hurston.

I'm pretty fuckin excited – we've got two introductory seminars this week and like –

This is the sort of thing I've been lookin forward to since I found out I got into uni

Like – chattin about books all day is *literally* heaven –

Better than heaven cos I'm *alive* and we're *still* chattin about books all day!

And I love this book so much so I'm mad excited to like break it down and chat it through.

The line goes inside and I find a seat.

The room's kinda small.

I look up and Emily's sat opposite.

'You alright?'

I say not knowin what to say

'Yeah'

Openin up her bag

Takin her laptop out

In silence

Not botherin to say nothin

Nothin to say

I look down at my books, look to my right

And then I notice –

I notice in the corner of the room there's a thin crack running down the seam of where the walls meet.

(*Yellow teeth, Australian accent.*) 'Sorry I'm late everyone!'

Our seminar leader bursts in.

'Hi! Hello! Shall we uh go round and say names?'

We're twenty minutes in

We've gone round, said names

Everyone's said where they're from and why they chose
   English, why they chose Bristol

I'm sat by the door and Barney's sat next to Emily and –

Wait I'm going too fast

Lemme describe

Lemme describe this dickhead yeah

It's only been twenty minutes and I already know this guy's a
   dickhead.

I mean we've probably all met a Barney right –

Home-counties-baby

Wearing-second-hand-everythin-so-we-don't-know-he's-rich

Mouth-perpetually-moving

Middle-parting-and-a-furrowed-brow-that-was-either-deep-
   thought-or-mad-constipation –

My money was on the latter.

Half the time's been taken up by him

His life story

His thoughts about the 'pursuit of knowledge'.

Our seminar leader –

Dry-skin-yellow-teeth

He's like

'So uh guys what did we think of the book?'

And straight away Barney starts chattin

'I mean, yeah the writing was just really relatable and raw and intimate and... it gave me this real sense of... I dunno if it was fear or... there was just this sense of unease... I liked it!'

And then he's like –

'It just felt really *BLACK*, you know, you could tell a *BLACK* woman wrote it, I mean the way it's just so...'

I'm lookin at him, and like what do I even say, what should I –

'I mean the way it just grabs you.'

The light's reflectin off his watch as he gestures and clutches at the air.

'This passage in particular'

He wets his lips and scans his crowd.

'It really struck me, when the grandma character, she's like –'

He bends the spine of his copy outta shape

He clears his throat.

'De nigger woman is de mule uh de world so fur as Ah can see'

He jabs his hand into the book.

'I love how it explores power structures and –'

'Yo, you can't say that'

'No I was just, I was reading the quote', he says in a fuckin patronisin voice

'Yeah man I know, but you can't say it, it's offensive'

And I'm lookin round the room

At his crowd

At the sea of white faces shiftin and swellin, lookin back at me

Like *I'm* mad.

'Offensive?'

'Yeah'

'What? Reading from a book?'

'Yes'

I say

Startin to doubt myself

'We'll agree to disagree on that one, bro', he says, grinnin

'Agree to disagree?' I say

I should've said, I'm not your fuckin bro

'Yeahhh I mean, you know, don't shoot me! But I don't think we should be giving words that much power over us'

'I think the radical thing is actually to take the power away from the words and just, you know, bring them to the table, call a spade a spade and have a conversation'

I should knock him out

'Literature's literature, like… it can't hurt us. Let's discuss!'

Two low-level thuds on the wall (like a heartbeat).

I flick my head to the crack in the wall as somethin strikes it twice from the outside.

Two low-level thuds on the wall (like a heartbeat).

'And I just think, sorry, but I think it's pretty illiberal to try and neuter a discussion about language because we're afraid of the language –'

Two low-level thuds on the wall (like a heartbeat).

'Like I get it in any other circumstance, *obviously*, but like, we're here to analyse?'

Two low-level thuds on the wall (like a heartbeat).

'We can't tiptoe around the object of our analysis. We've got to engage fully, surely?'

Two low-level thuds on the wall (like a heartbeat).

The sea of faces swells and smiles and stares, and Emily looks up and says –

Two low-level thuds on the wall (like a heartbeat).

'Yeah I do like actually like personally like get what you mean, like it's right here'

Two low-level thuds on the wall (like a heartbeat).

'De nigger woman is de mule uh de world so fur as Ah can see'

Two low-level thuds on the wall (like a heartbeat).

'And just like, being devil's advocate here, but if it says it, it says it, like… he didn't write the book?'

Two low-level thuds on the wall (like a heartbeat).

'Are you jokin?'

'It's just a discussion, you don't have to shout.'

Two low-level thuds on the wall (like a heartbeat).

She's looking at me, genuinely confused.

Two low-level thuds on the wall (like a heartbeat).

(*Seminar leader*) 'Okay great points everyone, nice debate. And I think Malik –'

'Malachi'.

Two low-level thuds on the wall (like a heartbeat).

'Yeah uh huh, I think the point that Barney and Em are making is a fair one, you know no one's saying it's a free-for-all, out there in the real world'

Two low-level thuds on the wall (like a heartbeat).

'But in here, we should really try and be a bit less sensitive, and
a bit more uh –'

Two low-level thuds on the wall (like a heartbeat).

'– objective, don't you think?'

And everyone starts agreein and my throat gets tight.

'That's not what I'm saying –'

(*Emily*) 'Yeah but it kind of is…'

Two low-level thuds on the wall (like a heartbeat).

I keep feelin these sideways looks. I'm tryna read their minds –
my thoughts intrudin.

Two low-level thuds on the wall (like a heartbeat).

Each fresh impact on the wall forms new fractures. Like
something's tryna get in.

Two low-level thuds on the wall (like a heartbeat).

Some guy with a *Pulp Fiction* top and bare spots, keeps starin
at me

Two low-level thuds on the wall (like a heartbeat).

I catch eyes with Emily

She flicks her eyes back to Barney

They keep at it

Having the discussion of their lives –

Chattin and debatin and I'm just sat there – silent

Lungs contractin, jaw tight.

Class ends –

I grab my shit, and head straight for the door

Down the corridor, take a left and –

(*Edinburgh accent*.) 'Hi!'

I turn around and it's that guy with the *Pulp Fiction* top who
 kept starin.

'What? What do you want?'

'No I just, um, I'm sorry, I should've –'

He's keeps fiddlin with the ring on his index finger, lookin bare
 sheepish.

'I just wanted to say that it wasn't cool, you know, how
 everyone was speaking to you in there, and aye, I just wanted
 to say that that was out of order, and check that you were
 okay', he says, kinda nervous laughin

'Yeah I'm fine, don't worry'

'Good, great, okay', he says, relief literally flooding his face

All the things he could've said in my defence surround us like a
 fog.

I wanna say

But you couldn't say anythin because, because what? Why?
 Fuck off.

But I don't

There's no point

I just say –

'Yeah, okay. See you tomorrow.'

'See you!', he says to my back as I head down the stairs

Flight after flight to the ground floor –

Breath tight.

The sound of scratching at the wall.

I wanna get out of this feeling

Press

This feeling

Pressin

This feeling

Pressin my fingers into my palms

Half-moon lines takin shape and it hurts.

People pass by me

I take a step back

Fade back

Breathe for a moment

Let my hands release

Reshape.

He breathes in.

He breathes out.

The scratching at the wall stops.

Okay.

***

I'm on a mission, man.

To get what I deserve

Find my people

Fall in love

And at the back of my mind I'm thinkin

Maybe a more realistic mission woulda been –

Operation 'Meet Some People Who at the Very Least Don't Talk
    to Me Like Shit'

But I'm not tryna give up.

I rifle through my bag

Pull out the guide I was circlin

Headin for these bright-white tents

Societies fair

Headin for uhhhh lemme see –

Stall twenty-three

Cut through crowds

Dodge the Mormons

Squeeze past groups and couples

Tryna make my way forward

Scan the stalls –

Rugby

Debating

Viking society

Beekeeping

Tantric yoga

Live-action role play

Twenty different a cappella groups

Then –

Right in the corner

Stall twenty-three –

Black Queer Society.

The stall's manned by one guy

Dressed in all black and

Shit

I can't even lie

He's actually fuckin leng

Crystal-clear skin and a mega-watt smile I guarantee could replace all the fossil fuels in this country

He looks me right in the eyes and my heart starts thuddin

Think of somethin clever

Think of somethin funny

Think of something clever *and* funny

'So

Uh

What do you

What's uh

This –'

The words come tumblin out before I catch them

The literal opposite of clever or funny

Askin what this is like it doesn't say Black Queer Society in fuckin block capitals right there

But he smiles and answers my question

Says it's Black Queer Society

He's the president, he's called Kojo, he's a second year

And the society is just a community basically

Place to socialise and meet and chat and hang out

And it sounds so sick

He asks me my name and I look in his eyes and it's like there are worlds inside them

'Where are you stayin?' he asks, and I find myself tellin him
    about last night – obviously redactin typhoid Michael stickin
    his tongue down my throat –

I tell him about the club and he laughs out loud – it's infectious
    – and he says everyone he knows has gotten trapped in a
    shrine to 'Mr Brightside' or 'Mr fuckin Blue Sky' aka the
    seventh circle of hell meets Fiat500 Twitter – at least once

And I laugh and he grins

I ask him what he does – while I freefall in his eyes and my
    heart beats faster

He does economics, but he plays piano – he's a composer

And I touch the corner of my mouth to make sure I'm not
    actually droolin.

I tell him I do English and he says that he used to read loads but
    wished he still did

'Well if you ever wanna pick it up', I offer, I can recommend
    you anythin anytime

And he's like – I'd actually love that

And I'm like 'Alright well poetry is basically lyrics anyway
    so I'd deffo recommend someone like T. S. Eliot – and
    like warning most of it's mainly about the hopelessness of
    humanity... but! It's so beautiful –'

'Right okay! Sounds fun!' He says laughin

'Nah trust me, just trust me'

'Alright I'll trust you! I'll read it', he says – and then he asks me
    if I'm free tonight

And I'm like uh I think so why

Restrainin myself from tellin him I literally could not be more
    free

And he tells me he's havin a party

If I wanna come

And I'm like –

'Definitely, I'd love that' – I'm tellin him I'll be there.

And I'm *gassed*.

***

It takes literally zero point nine seconds for my excitement to
   turn into stress

Cos I got no clue what to wear.

All I know is that I cannot under any circumstances

Look shit.

I get home and I start takin clothes out

Tryna decide what to wear

I've got this shirt

Or this shirt

Or this top

Or this top

Shades

Hats

Chains

Rings –

He changes clothes.

The tension rises.

He feels amazing.

I dunno if I believe in love at first sight

Like it's a myth right

But same time I dunno

Cos I'm mad restless to chat to Kojo

And I can just feel it

Fuck

This pull around my heart

Like –

I actually feel like I'm making up for lost time or something.

Cos no lie – three years ago, two years ago I wouldn't have even
    admitted it to myself, let alone anyone else

Like – at school? Even thinking that... no fucking way!

And sure yeah obviously there were some people, couple people

Came out bare early

Like they didn't give a fuck

Chargin through hostile territory – head high

But that could never be me

Wish it could

But

I dunno

I'm just sat in the corner

Every day tryna squeeze fantasies outta my head – skin crawlin

Like –

Looking back

It's a –

It's a weird thing –

Shame.

It's like it burrows through your marrow

Like an infestation

Roots deep and spreadin – diggin – feedin on a culture

At school

Everywhere to be fair

That makes you feel like actually physically sick to even
    imagine that you might be what you are.

And I'm just here tryna step through –

Every day lying

Hiding

Self-analysing

Code-switching

Hating

Cracking

Corroding

And what's left is just mad anxious – all the time.

At school, me and Femi spend what is pretty much every single
    wakin second together – like literally every day, no one else
    matters.

He comes out to me, I come out to him and we swear on
    everythin that we'll never tell a soul – fused in our secret

But even though it's a secret, my confidence is growin, my pride
    is growin, because of him, because I'm safe

And some days I look at him and then I look twice

And some days his hands brush past mine

And it's like that for ages like little looks, little touches, like
    nothing but everything at once.

And one day – we're cyclin.

***

We're cyclin fast – city blurrin past us

Fuelled on the promise of the bottle glowin in his Femi's bag
    that he's 'borrowed' from his older bro

We cycle up to the quietest, most covered part of the park

And I open the bottle up – cap spinnin through the air

He takes it off me, turns it vertical – gluggin –

And I'm like OKAY! PASS IT THEN!

And we sit and we chat and we drink

And the sun starts to set and he gets closer

And he smiles and time stops for a second and then he kisses
    me.

My heart is doin flippin somersaults – I've never kissed anyone in my entire life

I move back cos I'm nervous – I'm shook

Not cos I don't want it to happen

But because I want it to happen

And I dig my hands into the earth and amber coruscates and dances round his silhouette and I kiss him and I kiss him and I kiss him.

The world glides round its axis and the sun dissolves.

We walk back with our bikes

And we agree to keep it a secret cos it's not worth the hassle of everythin that comes with it not bein a secret.

The months soar by – every second together – and I feel like I've won the fuckin lottery

Until four weeks ago, one afternoon collides with time and stops it dead.

***

I'm in McDonald's queuing up

Strip lights searin lines into my eyes

Clutchin Femi's phone to get him a sweet chilli chicken wrap cos he's goin toilet

And I lift his phone up to pay and he gets a notification and the notification says 'three attachments' from Matt

And I'm like – huh?

I click it and my heart drops to my gut – head rushin – scrolling through a visual itinerary of this guy's body

I scroll up and see every part of Femi's body

And as I'm scrollin

Femi comes out the toilet

I tell him to come outside

I push down the twistin in my gut

I'm fucking pissed

'What the fuck is this?'

'What's what?'

'This – Femi. This'

I scroll up seein texts go back weeks

I can hear his pulse race I swear

He's like, they weren't doin anything in real life – they were just chattin –

And it's really startin to piss me off cos he's actin like I'm stupid, when he's fucked this guy

'You fucked him right? You fucked him?'

'I haven't fucked him'

'I know you fucked him, stop lyin'

'I haven't fucked him!'

'Oh right! So he fucked you! That's a first! Must be REALLY fuckin good then', I say, tryin and failin to keep my voice down – trust vanishin –

I look at him and he's screwin – defendin himself –

Tellin me to calm down

Refusin to admit he's fuckin bored or scared or horny – I don't even know – I don't care

I know he's fucked this guy

I can just feel my heart givin way – cold chill, throat tight, I cycle back

The twistin erupts, I throw up twice, my heart breaks like a
    detonation

Shrapnel in my gut –

I sit on the floor and I cry like a fuckin baby

And it hurts so much cos there's no one else –

Was no one else –

Through lyin, hidin, through fuckin… shame – there was no one
    else.

And I guess when you're on your own –

When there's only one raft –

Heartbreak hurts like grief.

My mum gets home and I tell her everything

I tell her everything I've not told her

And it's not a big deal for her at all – she just tells me that she
    loves me

Which just makes me cry even more

Because I know she means it

But that night –

I dream that I'm drownin for the first time

Thirty-one nights ago and every single night that follows.

Femi tries callin

Messagin

I block him on everythin

I spend every day readin – tunnel vision

Willin time to go forwards – forwards faster until I get to uni

Get here and meet someone who's actually excited by me

Someone better

And now I'm actually kinda thinkin that Kojo –

Kojo might be that person.

I've gotta chat to him again.

***

I wade through the autumn air

The breeze thick with recent rain

I'm nearly at Kojo's –

The sound of a heavy splash in the puddle behind MALACHI.
MALACHI *jumps*.

What the…?

MALACHI *looks to his sides and behind him.*

There's nothing there.

I walk faster.

***

I get there kinda late

And step inside a rush of sound and light

Scannin my eyes around the room.

The room's packed, everyone's in their groups and I've got no
    clue who to talk to

I'm frozen by the doorway, feelin kinda restless.

My hands are actually sweatin and I suddenly feel like mad
  nervous.

(*Grace*) 'Hey!'

This stunning Black girl comes up to me

She says her name's Grace

And I'm like

(*Awkward wave*.) 'I'm Malachi.'

And we hit it off straight away

She's from East and I start tryna convince her that West is better

Like did East even exist before 2012?!

She shakes her head and just says 'WOWWW'

But she's grinnin at the same time and I'm gassed the joke lands

A thud above MALACHI.

But I can't stop tryna figure out what's the right thing to say

If there's a right thing to say

How best to say it

A thud above MALACHI.

And I'm laughin and reactin on the outside

But my thoughts keep intrudin –

A thud above MALACHI.

MALACHI *looks up towards the sound – then spots Ade coming
up to him.*

This guy called Ade comes over and he talks like a million miles
  an hour

And even though we've just met he's actin like he's known me
   for so long – tellin story after story and I'm just stood there

Grinnin but my hands still sweatin

Kojo comes over and hugs me and my heart goes a bit faster and
   my mouth gets dry –

I just really wanna chat to him one on one

But Ade launches headfirst into tellin us about his night last
   night

'I wasn't even planning to go out!'

That's Ade –

'I wasn't even planning to go out! But this one here!'

He says pointing at Grace and she's like –

'You wanted to go out!'

Ade carries on –

'But *this one here* convinces me, and we all go out, whole group
   of us, and this guy – bare old – tries comin up to me while
   I'm at the bar tryna touch my bum. And like first of all –
   don't touch me. Second of all, please tell me why this man
   has like five teeth missing and has only got hair around the
   circumference of his head?!'

Kojo grins at me, opens his mouth like he's about to say
   somethin

But Ade's on a roll –

'In what flippin upside down is this guy coming near me,
   like move, man. Am I the Red Cross? Do I look like a
   humanitarian organisation? No! So don't come to me for
   charity, I beg!'

And everyone's laughin – I'm laughin

And I open my mouth to ask a question but at the same time
   someone changes the track

Music plays – 'Conceited (There's Something About Remy)' – Remy Ma.

And Kojo's like –

'OHHHHH SHIT! Nah I love this! Turn it up!'

And he starts dancin and Grace starts dancin and Ade starts dancin

The music gets louder and I look around

And the whole room erupts!

It takes like five seconds and every single body in the room is dancing so hard

Grace is literally crawlin on the floor

Ade's getting daggered by some girl

Kojo's next to me, dancing so well

Everyone is screamin

And the whole room looks *amazing*.

The music changes

Me and Kojo collapse on the sofa and he brushes my knee with his hand and leaves it there and my heart beats faster

He says he still owes me that piano lesson and I'm gassed he remembered

'Should I like message you maybe' I offer and he takes the bait with both hands and gives me his phone and asks me to put my number in – then he boasts he's read some T. S. Eliot

And I'm like what?!

I can't believe he actually read it, like full stop, let alone this quickly –

'You actually read it?'

He says 'Of course'

'I loved it. Like, don't get me wrong – yeah it's depressin! But it was beautiful at the same time. And it felt so much like music. Like shards of dissonance scattered through – notes that clash against each other, whose combination on the surface feels ugly or painful or not quite right, but a properly great composer knows how to take that pain and make it the most arrestin part of an entire symphony. And yeah, it just reminded me of that.'

He's fuckin amazing.

The sound of scratching at the walls.

But I can feel myself getting nervous

I look at the walls, and he asks what I'm lookin at

I look back at him, say it's nothin and try ignore it

My heart's beatin faster – breath tight chest tight – second guessin – sweatin –

I push it down and breathe and keep chattin.

The sound stops.

We talk and we drink

I'm kinda waved

He's smiling at me like he's kinda waved too – his eyes tracin my face –

And the music changes

And time stops

And I lean in

And I kiss him.

I kiss him and he kisses me back and my heart is racin.

I'm hopin so bad that he'll ask if I wanna stay the night so I can be like – uhhhhh YES YES OBVIOUSLY I WANNA STAY

THE NIGHT I'M ABOUT TO TELEPORT UPSTAIRS
RIGHT NOW! LET'S GOOOO!

But he doesn't ask which is cool cos it's too soon

But we talk for a couple more hours anyway and the chat is
    immaculate

And the night winds down

And I kiss him again and I leave.

***

I get back and I'm beamin from ear to ear

Like I literally cannot believe what just happened

And how much I want it to happen again

How much I wanna run back to his right now.

A little bit of hope cookin up inside me –

I never wanna stop feelin like this

Never wanna lose this

I think, and –

The sound of a thud above MALACHI.

MALACHI *looks up*.

*The groan of the ceiling, sagging underneath the weight of the
beast.*

I hear it again.

*The heavy sound travels across the ceiling as the beast searches
for a way into the room.*

The ceiling starts groanin like something so slow and heavy is
    pressin through its skin. Like something's treadin above

Circlin and circlin

A small cloud of plaster dust falls from the ceiling

And a hairline crack starts to form in the centre

And a single drop of water falls

Through the hairline crack onto my forehead and down my face

And then another

And another.

I go upstairs to investigate.

I head down the corridor

Up one flight of stairs

To the room directly above mine

But there's no name on the door

None of the doors

The whole floor's out of use.

I open the door to the room

But it's empty.

I step inside and on the carpet floor are wet, muddy marks

Like *THIS* big

I crouch down and touch the marks and they're freezing cold.

My mind's whirrin – tryna rationalise

I let the door shut

Back down the corridor

Down the stairs to my room

Lie down

Lock the door

I lock the door, close my eyes –

And sleep.

He takes a deep breath in and plunges into the depths of a dream.

***

MALACHI *is trapped in his bedroom at the bottom of the ocean.*

I'm drownin

I'm drownin

I'm drownin

I'm drownin

I'm drownin

I'm drownin

The world violently surges into darkness.

The rising cacophony of a hungry ocean, tearing through stone, metal, and bone.

The ceaseless banging of the beast on the walls of the room.

An iPhone alarm.

Then – the sun rises.

***

First thing in the morning and Kojo texts me like –

'Do you wanna get coffee later?'

And I was like –

I mean

You know when you don't wanna show that you're gassed
    right?

Obviously

Obviously you're GASSED

But you don't wanna show it

I'm tryna be cool

So I was just like

Yeah that'd be sweet

But I'm SO excited!

I spend the morning readin – passin time

I head out, I get there, I'm sat opposite him. And he looks
    incredible.

***

We're in this independent coffee place

Exposed bricks and pipes and I'm thinkin it must be the cost
    of removing all that plaster that makes this coffee so fuckin
    expensive.

We get chattin about music, politics, school, literally
    everything –

Every word he says I feel like bare comfortable and I just start
    to feel like I can trust him –

I tell him how I've found it being here and I'm ready for him to
    say how easy he found it – but he doesn't

He's honest

He's *honest* and he tells me –

'Me a year ago? I had *nothing* in common with a single one of
my flatmates! Like their *entire* personalities were ket, techno,
bags of wine, and *more ket*. And I tried soooo hard to fit
in – but they decided pretty quick they were *not* interested.
Wouldn't tell me about plans, stopped chatting when I came
in the kitchen to cook or whatever, and I wasn't tryna beg
it, so I stopped trying. And wasn't any better on my course
either, I literally spent every day of the first few weeks on my
ones, chatting to nobody. And it was hard, man. I was feeling
lower than I've ever felt in my entire life. Constantly. Second
guessing, feeling like a stranger, in the wrong place, at the
wrong time, with the wrong people. Just like mad isolated.
And I knew I wanted something different, but nothing was
gonna change with these people so – I went online tryna find
a society to join – nothing was speaking to me, but I was still
scrolling through all these random societies and I clocked
that I could fully just start my own. I did a call out on like
every single uni Facebook group, and got like five responses
total. Friday came around and three of the five didn't show.
But Grace and Ade – those two at the party – they did, and it
just kept growing, I have fully never looked back. Just kept
tryna take each moment as it comes I guess. And I've *never*
felt more free. So honestly, trust me. It's always hard. But it
gets easier.'

I'm listenin to him –

And I swear every word he says is like a blueprint

Cos the guy in front of me is mad confident

I'm lookin at him – listenin, and I swear I can feel hope racin
through me

Trust racin through me

I tell him what it means to hear what he's said and we just keep
chattin

And then I look at my watch and I'm running late for seminar so
I gotta say bye –

He tells me about another party at his tonight and I'm like uh
obviously I'll be there and then he leans in and he kisses me
and my heart skips and I hurry out into the pourin rain.

***

(*Barney*) 'Yeahhh so this is more of a comment than a question
but I was just *really* struck by the cultural power of the novel,
like the world is unrecognisable, obviously, but it was so
vivid!'

It's bucketin outside and I'm sat across from Barney

Lookin at his unbrushed tongue – flappin around and chattin shit

Emily's sat next to him basically brandin letters into her fingers
she's hittin the keys that hard

They're all clutchin identical white-and-burgundy cups

Cos they've all got a fuckin Pret subscription.

Everyone's here apart from Pulp Fiction guy – they're debating
the role of the language in the novel.

I just stare into space and try and fade it out

I try not to notice that there are more cracks in the corner of the
room

I try not to notice that it's like double more than last time

I only wanna think about one thing –

Kojo.

I can't stop thinkin about him

My eyes just glaze over –

And I'm floating

Levitatin, risin

Imaginin Kojo's holding me

Breathin deep

As we soar over creation

Mountains wide, valleys shinin

My heart risin to my head

We're airborne

Breeze underneath

As we rise like heat

Steam racin, spinnin

The earth rotates, time turns –

Wait.

We're stood still.

Fizzing

Hope racin through my blood.

Feelin stronger and stronger –

'I think it's fantastic how uncompromising the language is!'

Barney's voice breaks in –

(*Barney*) 'Like the dialogue's written in this kind of authentic *ethnic* dialect, and the first time you look at it, you're like – that's gibberish. But then you *dig*! You realise it's actually *radically* presenting the Black voice, and by extension, I suppose, the Black *body*, with this kind of tribal, ancestral authenticity. Like you can literally feel the Black girl sass coming off the page. It's amazing! It's palpable! And I wonder if –'

'What are you actually talking about?!'

Two low-level thuds on the wall (like a heartbeat).

The words charge out my mouth, strength movin through my veins –

Two low-level thuds on the wall (like a heartbeat).

'Literally *everything* you say, your entire analysis is so flawed it
would actually be funny if it wasn't so racist.'

Two low-level thuds on the wall (like a heartbeat).

'You're just slammin words together that you think make you
sound intelligent, but bro, it's doing the opposite. You're not
making sense. Your entire understanding of the author. Black
identity. The ways the novel negotiates language and power
and self – your understanding of all of it, is below zero. Just
shut up!'

Two heavy thuds on the wall (like a heartbeat).

I look to my right and my left

Where the walls meet

Two heavy thuds on the wall (like a heartbeat).

Where the thud of my thoughts intrude

Carvin cracks in the seams as the water spills in

Two heavy thuds on the wall (like a heartbeat).

Cos as the words cascade

I'm so glad I'm sayin them

But at the same time

Two heavy thuds on the wall (like a heartbeat).

Speakin up suddenly makes me feel more anxious than keepin
quiet did –

Even more anxious.

Barney's face turns scarlet

Opens his mouth but the clock hits the hour

Yellow Teeth moves us on, wraps it up –

Two heavy thuds on the wall (like a heartbeat).

I grab my stuff and I walk out – fast – heart drummin in my
chest

Heart drummin.

Two heavy thuds on the wall (like a heartbeat).

***

I go to the library

Tryna feel safe

Tryna find a couple books to read later

My heart still drummin.

I scan along the shelves

Flickin my eyes across titles and numbers.

Find one of the books I'm lookin for – pick it up and it's…

Soaking wet.

All the way through

Pages clogged and water runnin down its spine

But then I turn it over and –

It's dry.

The pages crisp and clean when it was wet one second ago.

I look up, run my eyes across the shelf, turn around and – there!

Right there!

Something flashin through the books –

I run around the shelf tryna see it properly

And I trip on the corner head-first into the next shelf

And the whole thing comes tumblin and hits the next and the
    next one comes crashin down

Books everywhere

And the librarian comes runnin and I'm like –

'Oh my god I am *so* sorry.'

But I'm lookin down and around surrounded by books

Pickin up shelves and placin books back and my thoughts –
    spinnin

Cos I read everything – classics, poetry, fiction –

But what I love most of all

Is fantasy… sci-fi…

And in the books I love –

The supernatural is possible and the impossible is natural and
    life teeters on the edge of the unreal

And now my mind is properly racin – tryna piece together what
    I've seen

And I start to wonder –

If something strange is happening

Something I can't explain

Something fantastic in the most terrifying way like in all the
    books I've read since I could read.

And obviously I know how that sounds

But things keep happening.

Things keep happenin that I can't explain.

I keep seein – hearin things I can't explain

There was something round that shelf

On the way to Kojo's, in the seminar, in my room, at the party...

There's something in the corner of my eye – hunting – and it's
    close and wet and cold and hungry.

***

I move fast through heavy rain

Steppin through wide puddles

Swervin empty bottles and movin down the street

Water drippin down my neck

Questions runnin through my mind I can't answer.

I walk past an electronics shop with screens piled high

Deep in the window

Fourteen squares burnin news on the hour into the air

Ticker tape runs red along the bottom –

Climate crisis, justice hopes wages – sinkin – but also – '*Strictly*
    next week!' – tagged on the end

Placin a cherry on top of an inferno

My chest gets tighter.

I keep walkin

But I hear something shiftin –

In the distance getting closer

I speed up –

Keep movin forwards

I look back

I look back and in the corner of my eye I see a shiftin mass
chargin towards me

It's fuckin chasin me down

I run as fast as I can –

I keep runnin

It's poundin after me

I keep runnin

It's poundin after me

I keep runnin – it's comin faster and faster

Head down, I run – heart racin.

I get in

I close the bedroom door behind me

I lock it

Breathe

Press press

Breathe

Half-moon lines takin shape – it hurts

Breathe

A VERY, VERY LOUD BANGBANGBANG.

It keeps comin –

BANGBANGBANG!

Pounding like heavy artillery in my head – like a fuckin Gatling
gun –

BANGBANGBANG!!

Tryna break down the wall

Tryna break down the wall between nightmare and reality

And it's bucklin

The wall's bucklin

As the beast claws its way outta my dreams.

BANGBANGBANG!!

I reach round the back of my bed – I push it I slam it against the
    door tryna shut the beast up.

And then I notice

Under my bed

In the corner of the room

The carpet is frayin and comin up

And something makes me look closer.

I reach round the fraying edge and it all comes up

 ᶜ Under my bed, under my desk, round the room and underneath –

The carpet's coverin bars and bars of rusted metal and cracked
    concrete

The foundation's waterlogged – algae in the cracks

Shiftin pockets of blue pirouette and shimmer through pitch-
    black

Reality starts to rot and fester at my feet cos I know where I am

I know where I am

I'm in my bedroom

My bedroom at the bottom of the ocean

I'm in my bedroom at the bottom of the ocean

The light starts turnin

My stomach starts turnin tryna rationalise the impossible –

Reality bleedin red into my dreams

My soul threaded through cavin walls and monsters' teeth –

I race towards the door

I open the door and water gushes through

And in its wake –

The beast climbs in.

I look into its eyes and it looks into mine

Blowin hot wet air across my cheeks

Acid drippin from six rows of teeth and oh my god it's real

It's real

It's real.

I try and run past it, get to the door – but it blocks my way

And I'm tryna keep my breath steady

But it's like

It feels like my heart

My mind is is is

Hot plastic –

Mouldin round the ridges of its grip

Bendin round its fist – I can't slip out

I can't get out into the air – its grip

Its grip's mutatin me –

There are worlds and waves and dread and dreams fallin
   through my fingers – and I can't keep up –

He breathes in.

He breathes out.

I think of Kojo and I breathe

And hope floods through my veins

The possibility of what might be

Rushin through my mind

Fizzin

Steam racin

The possibility to trust someone

Maybe even love someone

Hope surges ultraviolet through my marrow – dissolvin fear

And I look down –

And a flaming sword forms in my grip.

I lift the sword above my head and hack down into its jaws

It screams, I hack again, it screams

I shove the jagged edge into its thick gut and wrench my arms
   up until its insides spit

I smack it across the face

I smack it again

I smack it again

I duck behind it.

It turns its bloodied heads towards me bearin six rows of teeth

I bend its spine outta shape, ripping tissue, breakin bone as
   liquid flesh falls around me

I peel back its ribcage piece by piece

I shove my hand into its chest and pull out its pumpin heart

I dash its heart against the wall

It drops down – rottin in the blue

It's dead

It's fuckin dead!!!

I climb over it and through the door – I run

I brace myself to hit the ocean but reality reasserts itself

And my feet touch the corridor floor.

I race down the street

Through the settin sun all the way to Kojo's

Movin through the fresh air and it feels so good to get out and
  breathe.

I am not fallin down

Rottin

Runnin out of time or out of light

I'm not dreamin or already drowned

Sinkin or already sunk

I'm alive, man!

And I know the beast might come back

I know that

I get that.

But one day at a time

I'll keep breathin –

Hope in my lungs.

I get to his door

I knock on his door

Ready to step inside a rush of sound and light

And be as brave as I possibly can

Try take each moment as it comes – just above the waves.

I see him gettin closer through the glass

Lamp light glowin round his silhouette

And the door opens

It opens

Deep breath –

'Hi'.

The End.

Other Titles in this Series

A Nick Hern Book

Dreaming and Drowning first published in Great Britain as a paperback original in 2023 by Nick Hern Books Limited, The Glasshouse, 49a Goldhawk Road, London W12 8QP in association with WoLab and the Bush Theatre

Dreaming and Drowning copyright © 2023 Kwame Owusu

Kwame Owusu has asserted his right to be identified as the author of this work

Cover image by Joel Omolo

Designed and typeset by Nick Hern Books, London
Printed in Great Britain by Mimeo Ltd, Huntingdon, Cambridgeshire PE29 6XX

A CIP catalogue record for this book is available from the British Library

ISBN 978 1 83904 304 8

www.nickhernbooks.co.uk/environmental-policy

www.nickhernbooks.co.uk

facebook.com/nickhernbooks

twitter.com/nickhernbooks